ACTIVE
PRAYER
SERIES

Making Crosses

Ellen Morris Prewitt A Creative Connection to God

PARACLETE PRESS
BREWSTER, MASSACHUSETTS

Making Crosses: A Creative Connection to God

2015   Fifth Printing
2012   Fourth Printing
2011   Third Printing
2010   Second Printing
2009   First Printing

Copyright © 2009 by Ellen Morris Prewitt

ISBN: 978-1-55725-628-7

Unless otherwise indicated, Scripture quotations are taken from *The Revised English Bible.*
Copyright © Oxford University Press and Cambridge University Press, 1989. All rights
reserved. Reprinted by permission.

Scripture quotations designated KJV are taken from the Authorized King James Version of the
Bible.

Noted prayers are taken from *The Book of Common Prayer,* published by the Church Hymnal
Corporation, New York, in 1979.

Library of Congress Cataloging-in-Publication Data

Prewitt, Ellen Morris.
  Making crosses : a creative connection to God / Ellen Morris Prewitt.
    p. cm.—(Active prayer series)
  ISBN 978-1-55725-628-7
  1. Crosses. 2. Prayer—Christianity. 3. Spiritual life—Christianity. I. Title.
  BV160.P74 2009
  246'.558—dc22   2009000900

10 9 8 7 6 5

Published by Paraclete Press
Brewster, Massachusetts
www.paracletepress.com
Printed in the United States of America

Contents

Part 2
Other Things
You Might Want to Know

Appendix
Supplies and Tips
for Individuals and Groups

Introduction

I began making crosses after our country was hit by the tragedy of September 11, 2001. With my heart torn in two, I needed to do something that mattered. I turned to the cross. At the time, I did not know why I made such a choice, but now I do: the cross is a source of infinite understanding. Wherever you are in your life—in the dark of Good Friday or the light of Easter morning, holding on to the hope of salvation or attempting to follow the impossible requests of the Savior, mourning Christ's unjust death or celebrating His unjustified gift of life—the cross holds the answers you need. I have found that to be true.

As with all crosses created in prayer, my crosses are unique creations that express my relationship with God. I begin by finding something as simple as two sticks. I bind the sticks together into crossbeams. I then adorn the cross with broken and found objects from the world around me—scraps of metal shining on the sidewalk, singleton earrings, keys lying forgotten in my garage. I select objects that speak to me in ways that sometimes I can't quite explain when I first begin to work on the crosses. Whether they represent symbols of Christianity, themes and stories from the Bible, or Jesus of Nazareth Our Savior, the adornments come together to express my communion with God.

In conducting cross-making workshops, I've found that all—even those who think they can't—make wondrous crosses. By making crosses I am better able to understand what God needs for me to understand about myself, my church, or whatever may be working in my life. To make a cross is to pray in a new way that is very different from old-fashioned petitionary prayer; making crosses is a way for God to pray *through* you.

This book is about the new spiritual practice of making crosses and how it can transform your relationship with God, yourself, and the world around you.

The building blocks of cross making are quite simple:

1 Take what the world doesn't value and make it into a work of God.

2 Reject the materialism of this world, in your own small way, by reusing discarded materials and giving them new, godly life.

3 Engage in an activity that takes you directly into communion with God.

The practice of cross making is for those who want to experience God beyond their day-to-day prayers. Often, we feel so strongly a need to be with God in a special way, but we can't find the time to make that connection. Or, when we do make time, our thoughts drift too easily from prayer to worrying to random speculation, or we simply begin planning activities for the next day.

Let's prepare ourselves to engage in a new, different, artistic practice.

Making crosses is a "way of more." More than the oral or written word, more than our analytical thinking, making crosses is a way of understanding that comes from doing. And doing with our hands. Making crosses locates you in a place of prayer and keeps you there. As you work on the crosses, God is right there beside you, making suggestions, leading you into new understandings, showing you things that you didn't know you knew. Because you are working on the most complex symbol of Christianity—the cross—you are attached deeply to God. And, as with all good spiritual practices, cross making allows you to turn your revelations outward as you share in communion with others. Cross making is an activity that invites community. If you can, find a friend who will share in this new practice with you.

The cross making itself is physically simple, but it takes some spiritual preparation. Let's prepare ourselves to engage in a new, different, artistic practice.

Part 1
A Creative Way of Prayer

1 Trying Something New

Through conducting cross-making workshops, I have found that many of us shy away from expressing our love of God through creativity because we feel that our creations are not worthy. We question whether our feelings for God—love, awe, gratitude, worship—are good enough. And yet, almost all of us have had a moment when we knew that God loved us and knew it deep inside our being and stronger than we ever had before.

As we embark on a new creative venture, it helps to remember that we are working with a God who loves us more than anything in the world. For me, this experience of God's immense love occurred one day when I was greatly missing my little dog, Lucy. I never had children; Lucy was the tiniest of my three dogs, the one I protected and kept safe from harm's way, but no one from the middle part of my life understood how I felt about Lucy, and they dismissed this love. One day, in the faint stirrings of summer's heat, I was walking the driveway of the house where Lucy spent her last days. In the midst of my sorrowing for little Lucy, I heard a voice say, "I will give her back to you."

I knew this voice belonged to God and I knew what he meant: when I died and arrived in heaven, Lucy would be given back to me. God loves me, I loved Lucy, and that was that. I had never experienced anything so loving. God did not judge my love for Lucy and find it wanting. God knew my heart's desire and it was his joy to give it to me. This loving relationship with God I now carry with me into the rest of my life, and especially into my spiritual practices.

When I'm making crosses, I open up my mind. I let myself be led wherever I need to be led. I know that God will lead me to new places that I could not have found on my own, revelatory places that will tilt the way I currently look at my world. I know I will find understanding deep inside myself that I did not know was there. And, in the process, I will experience God's immense love—the "peace that passes all understanding." Inside this peace, it is my joy to play and create, and re-use and mess with and stumble across and transform each cross from vision to visual reality. My joy matters. And it is being given to me.

Who would have ever thought that my heart's desire—me, a woman who cannot draw a straight line, who spent the dominant portion of her life carrying a briefcase—would be found in creating crosses from discarded bits of brokenness? I've seen this same surprise in others, too, during cross-making workshops. It is a revelation, their joy as they spend time with their newly found crossbeams, contemplate their broken treasures, and piece it all together in ways revealed to them while they reflect on what it means to be a child of God.

There are aspects of ourselves that we cannot see clearly. We must trust God to take care of us, for God knows us fully. He knows what things lie at the center of our heart's desire, but outside our limited field of vision. As the psalmist said, "Lord, you have examined me and you know me. You know me at rest and in action; you discern my thoughts from afar. You trace my journeying and my resting-places, and are familiar with all the paths I take. For there is not a word that I speak but you, Lord, know all about it" (Ps. 139:1–4).

Trust God. Trust the One who knows the secrets of our hearts and whose joy it is to give them to us:

That we may perfectly love you, and worthily magnify your holy Name; through Christ our Lord. Amen.

(*Book of Common Prayer*, The Holy Eucharist: Rite Two, 355)

Trust the One who knows the secrets of our hearts and whose joy it is to give them to us.

Exercise

Think about a moment or moments when you have experienced God's most profound love: "For God so loved the world" (Jn. 3:16). Relive the sense of peace and security and happiness this experience brought to you. In the Notes section that follows, write directly onto the pages of this book the words that best describe how you felt. Set yourself in that place, so that for the time you are making crosses you are speaking to that God, the One who loves you so.

Notes

2 Whatever We Do, God Can Work with It

We are all put together differently. What gives me comfort might make you uncomfortable. Sometimes in workshops when I say, "There is no right way to do this," I think folks actually hear, "There is *no* way to do this." What was supposed to be a comfort—your work will not be judged as right or wrong—is heard as a total lack of structure. Whatever our makeup, the key to proceeding in peace—as with all aspects of cross making—is to bring God into the picture. Once there, God can work with anything.

"There is no such thing as a mistake." That's what I have to tell myself in cross-making, since my inner critic can be so strong. To handle my fear, I have told myself that whatever I do in the process of creating a cross is simply what it is; it is a process, and God is very much in it every step of the way. With my focus thus on God, I consider what I have placed on my cross. If it is not saying quite what I am feeling, I do not rip it up and start over. I accept it for what it is, and I add to it to get closer to where God wants me to be.

*Don't worry,
everything can be
salvaged.*

Once you adopt this attitude, you let go of undoing. Nothing on the cross gets taken apart and put together in a different way. In other words, the standards of cross making are not those of an art project. Many real artists will repaint an entire portion of a canvas, erasing their first drafts as if they never existed. This ability to redo their work twenty-five times if necessary to get it "just right" might give some folks comfort, but "right" can also quickly become an impossibly high standard. Comfort arrives from the fact that you do not have to get it right. Always remember: God wants our attention, not our perfection.

I try to keep this principle in mind in other parts of my life as well, because I hate doing something that I later regret. Whether it's losing my temper, saying something ugly, or looking the other way when someone needs my help, I fall short more often than not. And no matter how much I want to undo my actions, I can't.

But I can add to them; I can fill out the picture and make it better.

Maybe God has the same attitude. Maybe long ago our Lord and Creator gave up any idea that we would return to the perfection of Genesis where we were created male and female in God's own image. Maybe our seemingly steadfast inability to meet God's high standards forced God to say, "Here's what I will do: I'll broaden the picture. I'll send you my Son, and he will show you the way. You just aren't getting the teachings, the words, so I'll give you a life. Follow my Son and, step by step, you will return to this earth the kingdom of God."

As we trot through life, paying varying degrees of attention to our actions and the world around us, we will keep missing the mark; it is our nature. But God's motto is, "Don't worry, everything can be salvaged. Whatever you do, we'll work with it."

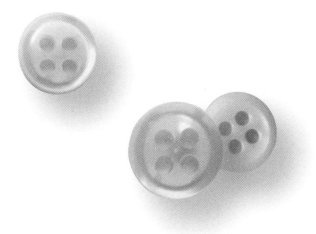

Exercise

Meditate on what it means to you to be a co-creator with God. That is what you will be doing in cross making: creating something new together with God. In what other aspects of life have you felt you were a co-creator with God? Using your prayer thoughts, make a list in the Notes section of creation goals that do not include the word *perfection*. Read your list out loud, either to yourself or the friend who is on this cross-making journey with you. Adopt it as your roadmap to co-creation, understanding that whatever happens in life, you are already forgiven.

Notes

3 Getting Started

Everything in cross making is done for a reason. It might not be a reason that makes sense to this world, but cross making is an ongoing, intentional process of making prayerful decisions. These decisions undergird everything we do, and over time they come to form our paths for this spiritual practice.

My cross-making inspiration comes from God's word: take what the world doesn't value and use it to commune with God, or "So the last will be first, and the first last" (Mt. 20:16). Again: reject the rampant materialism of this world, or "Sell all that you have, give to the poor, then come and follow me" (Lk. 18:22).

My methods of cross making are homemade; they came to me through doing. For example, I cannot destroy perfectly good material to use in cross making. I discovered this truth as I was tearing apart a warped picture frame. I whacked the frame with a hammer, loosening joints and exposing small rusty nails. I hit it again. The hammer thudded and the wood splintered. A section of the frame dangled free. I would nail this section to another section, and there would be my crossbeams. But this frame was only available to me because, for a while, I had tried to frame my crosses using old picture frames. It hadn't worked, and the old frames cluttered my cross closet.

Then one day, I saw them as potential cross beams and began using them. But what would happen when I ran out? Could I scour flea markets and buy more frames, knowing I would rip them apart? It didn't seem right to me. And so I added to my cross-making philosophy: You cannot destroy for your own cross-making purposes. Wait; what you need for the crosses will come.

As you work on your crosses, *your* governing standards will be developed by you and God together. These standards will likely be different from mine, or from those of the others with whom you share this practice. That's OK. Embrace your rules. After all, when Jesus sent his disciples into the world, he gave them rules to follow: "'Take nothing for the journey,' he told them, 'neither stick nor pack, neither bread nor money; nor are you to have a second coat'" (Lk. 9:3). While the substance of the rules was important (so that the disciples didn't swoop into villages and lecture the locals, but instead arrived dependent on the villagers' hospitality), the fact of the rules was equally essential. Similarly, the strictures of cross making transform it into a religious undertaking, something done with intention.

For me, crosses cannot be separated from what they symbolize: a rejection of the world's way of valuing. That is why I try to use only broken, discarded, seemingly worthless objects. I admire crosses made with gold or jewels or fine things, but I cannot work that way. It's the very commonness of the cross materials—a plumber's elbow, found string, a broken key chain—that, for me, helps the meaning of the cross itself to come through. The simplicity removes religious pretense and spiritual smugness and points instead to the everyday fact of the cross.

So much of what we humans release into this world becomes a permanent part of creation, hanging around in the parking lot or on the sidewalk, washed up on the shoreline. And even though our discarded objects have long since become useless to us, they are still beautiful. In my cross making, I want to use that which is unvalued by the world, unnoticed even, to make images of God: "Things which were cast down are being raised up" (*Book of Common Prayer*, Final Solemn Collect of Good Friday, 280). The crosses are the carpenter Jesus's crosses, the embodiment of all that Jesus told over and over again in the parables when he said: do not listen to the world, do not think the way the world thinks, do not get caught up in unrighteous mammon. Work with me.

Cross making is an ongoing, intentional process of making prayerful decisions.

17

As you work with Jesus in making your own crosses, your passion will break through and shape how you decide to proceed. Your dedication to making a godly home may limit your objects to items you can find in your house. "Finding" for you may mean you do not amend anything from its original found state: no further breaking of broken pottery, no bending or twisting, no refolding. Your dedication to simplicity may render your crosses very plain and direct. Many of the crosses that we create in cross-making workshops are nothing more than found crossbeams wound together with found crossties. They are stark, compelling.

Your crosses are the physical manifestation of your immersion in God. When you look on them, you will remember when God was so close beside you. And God, watching your struggles, will say, "Finally, you have turned your heart to me."

The Blessed Assurance

With God beside me,
I cannot worry about what others will think of my beliefs.
I will not clam up in fear and refuse to speak to you
about my time with God.
Together, in His name,
we will approach a place
that isn't quite where we were before.
As we make crosses,
we will carry with us the Blessed Assurance:
we are not as alone as we think we are.

Exercise

On a separate piece of paper, make a list of attributes you feel others consider "religious." In the Notes section that follows, make a list of the attributes you consider "religious." Don't be afraid to include points that are yours and yours alone. When you are finished, tuck your first list between these pages and mentally set the two lists aside. Once you have completed your first cross, return to the Notes section and make a list of what you felt as you worked on the cross. Be specific about what was important to you. Compare this list to the list of attributes you consider religious. What do you see? Now tear up the list of what others consider religious. Tear it up into little pieces.

Notes

4 Step One: Find Two Sticks

The first step in making crosses is to find your crossbeams. These can be found anywhere—in your yard, on the street, in your garage, or by the seashore. All you need to get started, in some form or fashion, is two sticks. As you select your sticks for your crossbeams, remember: everything you do in cross making is a revelation from God. That means some of it may not make sense to you at first. You may feel led to do something a certain way and not know why. That's good. Follow it. Be guided by the Holy Spirit, trusting in your blindness that light will break through.

Don't be surprised if the revelation of your cross making seeps into other aspects of your life as well. One time during Holy Week, when the crosses in my church were draped in cloth, the priest spoke to us about acknowledging Jesus in our lives. As I took in his words, I studied the cloth-covered crosses and I was calm—I had no involuntary cringe at my failure to claim our Savior, none of my usual guilt at my own timidity. The moment slid by without anxiety.

You cannot work on crosses
without your love of God expanding,
then exploding into the public arena.

What caused the change? I don't know, but I do know this: you cannot work on crosses without your love of God expanding, then exploding into the public arena. It's a drip process: drip, drip, drip. A slow, steady, almost plodding erosion of hesitancy, self-consciousness, embarrassment. Like water against stone, like love against a hardened heart: nothing is more ongoing than the everyday transformation of the cross.

Our yearning as humans is for "once and done." "Give us this day our daily bread," we pray. But what we really mean is, fill our pantry full. We want the security now, the goodness now, the answer now—peal of thunder, crack of lightning! Abracadabra! Presto-chango! We long for a big moment of revelation when we're zapped by goodness, and then, ever after, are God's precious angels of light.

But we're not angels, and neither are others. "Seventy times seven," Jesus said (Mt. 18:22), and we see ourselves forgiving myriad of different transgressions, but what I think he meant was that, for the most part, you will be forgiving the same person for the exact same behavior over and over and over again. Understanding—our own understanding, the understanding of others—arrives swaddled in time, delivered over the years. But just because it arrives piecemeal, doesn't mean it's not a revelation.

Exercise

Your sticks seem very simple and, in one way, they are. But simple doesn't mean we don't need God to be a part of the process, and that's true especially in our cross-making practice. Your sticks will set the mood for your cross. If they are curvy, your cross will proceed with movement. If you trim the sticks to make them straight and formal, your cross will begin with that temperament. How will you know the type of cross God wants you to make today if you don't ask God to help you consider your crossbeams?

Objects I have used as crossbeams:

Dowels from a rotted front porch
Antique shutter louvers
Warped picture frames
Pipes from a broken wind chime
Legs from a broken table
Slats from a beach rocker
Twined grapevines
Scrap fabric stuffed with newspaper
Chicken wire
Beaded board
Bamboo
A broken balsa wood box
Yellow glass
Garden edging
Driftwood

Objects I have seen others use as crossbeams:

Old candles
Railroad nails
Discarded wood
Sticks from the yard
Needles
Pencils
Plywood
Found lumber
Popsicle sticks

Notes

5 Step Two: Holding It Together

After you've selected your crossbeam sticks, you must decide how to hold the sticks together. Choices abound. Will you wire them, or tie them with twine, or wind string around them? The way you bind your crossbeams is an essential part of the spiritual practice of cross making because it mirrors the hard choices we face in life. When faced with such choices, we must ask ourselves: Do we turn to things of this world—eat too much, drink too much, worry too much—or do we turn to God? How do we ultimately decide to hold it together?

Cross making is simple, but anything new can be frustrating. In particular, your fingers may feel clumsy as you try to wind your sticks with wire. When you bump up against the gap between your idealized vision of what a cross is "supposed to look like" and the earthy reality of a cumbersome new task, you may be tempted to give up. When frustration rises, the will to continue can dry up and blow away. We can so easily convince ourselves that it wasn't that important anyway, and our kids are calling for attention, and what were we thinking trying to make such a complicated cross in the first place?

This is the exact time when you need to hold it together. Because on the other side of this rough patch lies revelation. Remember: As you engage in this practice, you are experiencing a new kind of prayer. Talk with God as you go.

Go slowly. When you find yourself frustrated, relax.

Recognize that in your cross making a time will come when the very things you depend on—the plastic, slippery fishing wire that tends to unknot itself like a worm sliding off the hook, the tube of invisible but impregnable glue that never seems to dab where it's supposed to dab, the latex gloves that flop right into the spot you are trying to work on—will drive you up the wall.

That's okay. Go slowly. When you find yourself frustrated, relax. Take a breath. Remember God. And remind yourself:

My fishing line is a miracle product.

My glue is perfect for what I need.

My latex gloves are brilliantly protective.

And pray: Lord, in your mercy, save us from ourselves.

Exercise

Are you feeling frustrated as you work to create your crossbeams?
Write down your feelings in the Notes section. Be specific. Don't
fudge or clean up your language. God will use your honesty as
an opportunity for revelation as well.

Suggestions for Binding Your Crossbeams

The easiest way to bind your sticks is to wire them. You can use new wire from the hardware store or found wire. Once, when I was wondering where on earth I'd get enough wire to create a set of crosses, I stumbled across an abandoned burn site with leftover, unburned wire—if you want to use found wire, you just might find it. A good pair of scissors can cut the light gauge of wire that is usually sufficient for making a cross. For anything heavier, use wire clippers. Your cross has begun.

Notes

6 Struggling with Spirituality in Cross Making

Sometimes, because of where we are in our spiritual lives, we are drawn to use two very simple sticks in our prayer of making a cross. At other times our spiritual struggles are more involved, and the cross we need to make requires more than two simple sticks. If you realize this need before you begin collecting for your cross, then look for your crossbeams among the more substantial materials that abound in the world. If, however, you don't come to this realization until you are seated at your cross table and your cross making is underway, follow the directions on page 39 to wind a handful of your simple sticks into a sturdier crossbeam. Similarly, your lighthearted joy in God might need more color to express itself, a more exuberant backing. If so, turn to the directions on page 40 for trimming your crossbeams in tissue paper. Whatever you need, be flexible and allow the Holy Spirit to take you in new directions. What is God saying to you about himself, about *yourself*, in the way that you are creating this cross?

Most of the time, I do not come to my cross table with a problem to be solved, a riddle to be answered. I come to the table to be with God, and as I work, God comes to be with me. A thought will slowly form and take hold. Then, as I begin to transform the

Don't worry about a roadmap or set pattern.

thought into something physical, I am forced to consider what exactly I meant by that thought. At this point, I ask and ask and ask—it is not my working out of things that matters, but God's.

With God by my side, I have worked away from the male-dominated imagery of our church and into God the Creator, God the Savior, and God the Spirit. I have worked out my horror at the violence done to Jesus in a cross where the hands and feet of our Lord are staples that once held my broken soaker hose in place and the crown a broken Christmas ornament. I have worked out my frustration at our refusal to remember the living, breathing Christ by honoring him with a manger made from a plumber's elbow and nails that are carpet tacks. I have worked out my repeated failures to live up to the person God wants me to be by creating a confession cross with rusted iron designed to be removed during the confession process and replaced . . . removed again, replaced.

If the Spirit moves you into a more joyful place, go with that. Don't worry about a roadmap or set pattern. Much of the beauty in our lives depends, I believe, on unintentionality. I see this truth in church each Sunday, in the threads of our lives as woven together by God: the middle-aged man with the bad hip who roils down the aisle like a sailor, followed by the skipping little boy with the aberrant red-headed gene, he who is so gentle. The prayer we say each Sunday without fail—"Our Father, Who art in Heaven"—is plural, a prayer of commonality. We claim that we as a church are one body in his

*. . . do whatever
the Holy Spirit leads
you to do.*

name—gathered at the altar, knitted into pews, pleated in choir robes, and smocked in Easter finery. Together, we kneel and become a beautiful, mysterious pattern.

A cross that you approach without a set agenda—an unintentional cross—can sometimes communicate these mysterious patterns of our lives best of all. Take a fresh look at the crosses that you have made up until this point; you may see that they show patterns of spiritual issues you are working on, issues that perhaps you didn't even realize you were working on when you first made them.

It may be that your spiritual struggles lead you to combine your cross making with other spiritual practices. For example, you might want to walk the labyrinth, then settle in at your cross table to clarify and express your experience. Or, following your study of Scripture, you can turn to cross making as a way to expand and deepen the insight you've received. Cross making is also a good way to complement a period of meditation: quiet, centering prayer, followed by quiet, physical prayer.

Wherever you are, begin there. Then, as in all things in making crosses, do whatever the Holy Spirit leads you to do.

Exercise

If you want to make a more formal, heavier cross, divide your sticks into two groups of four or five sticks each. Lay one group of sticks in a horizontal direction on a flat surface. Take your wire and, toward the left end of the group, attach the wire to the first stick by wrapping. Then weave the wire in and out of the remaining sticks (over one stick, under the next, over the next). Return, backtracking in the same manner, to the first stick. Repeat this on the right end of the group. When you finish, you'll have a crossbeam that lies flat. Repeat for the second group of sticks and bind the two crossbeams together. But . . . do not be constrained by these directions. Assemble your cross in any way that comes to you; I have had workshop participants make three-dimensional crosses. You must let the Holy Spirit take you where it will. If the material you have chosen as your crossbeams is larger or heavier than regular sticks—such as old picture frames or scrap wood—glue them together first. Let the glue dry, then bind them with wire.

Decorating Your Cross with Tissue Paper

If your cross needs a base of color, consider decorating it with tissue paper.

1 Gather reclaimed or purchased tissue paper. Tear the tissue into long, thin strips.

2 Mix Elmer's glue and water in a small pan until it achieves the consistency of egg whites.

3 Trail the tissue through the glue/water.

4 Wrap the wetted tissue onto your crossbeams. Layer the tissue in the same way you would paint a wall, with overlapping strokes. The tissue will primarily stick to other tissue, not the wood of the crossbeam, so end your stroke with tissue on tissue. Scrunch the tissue if you want to add a crinkle effect and depth.

5 If the tissue is unusually thin, instead of trailing it through the glue, dab your little finger into the glue/water and pat that onto the paper.

6 Repeat the above until you've achieved the look you want. Some color combinations—such as red on white—will bleed. If this happens, make martyrs' crosses.

7 Let the glued tissue dry overnight. If you want more permanency, spray with a fixative, shiny or dull, outdoors where the fixative odor can dissipate. Let the tissued cross rest while you prepare yourself for adornment.

Notes

7 Step Three: Collecting for Your Cross

To make a cross, we must slow down. We must reconsider our everyday, absolutely routine actions, such as throwing something away. In the ordinary world, we snatch and toss. In the cross world, we stop and examine. As we collect objects to adorn our crosses, we pause, we observe. We set aside the materialistic values of the world and let the Holy Spirit open our eyes to a different way of seeing the things of creation.

To begin your collecting, declare a "Cross Collection Week." Throughout that week, when you find yourself with something in hand to throw away, stop. Consider: could this be cross material? You will be amazed at how much of what you would otherwise toss turns out to be perfect for a cross:

- The tissue paper casually stuffed into the mouth of your shopping bag is perfect for coloring your cross;
- The thin ribbon that ties the handles of a gift bag together will easily become a crosstie;
- Even the red plastic cell phone cover—its trough is a manger crying out for a baby Jesus.

I often ask participants to have a Cross Collection Week before we have our workshop. Participants have brought in wine bottle covers, stripped silver foil, vintage paper, broken glass—all sorts of things. Other odd things I've used in crosses include a ruined pair of leotards, drink stirrers, the wishbone from the Thanksgiving turkey, pages from old family books that were about to be thrown away, and smushed beer caps, which make wonderful halos. Everything can become material for a cross.

Why, you might ask, don't we just go to a store and buy what we need for the crosses? Because we already have on hand what we need, and to purchase more would be an extravagance when cross making is an exercise of utmost simplicity. If we make a shopping list, we begin thinking "decoration," and the chances are too high that God will slip from the process. We want to look for God everywhere in the world; we do not want to seek only in places that money can find.

Look for God everywhere in the world.

"Scrounging" is an even more dramatic example of turning to worthless clutter of this world for your materials. To scrounge, look down, a place where you might not usually look. If you spy a rusted washer in a parking lot, pick it up. (I'm not exactly sure what the original purpose of a washer is, but they are round metal things with a hole in the middle that seem to be universally discarded; workshop participants bring them in all the time.) Never stop to ask yourself what you will do with what you pick up. Trust your brain—not your analytical mind, but the part of your brain that allows God entry when you aren't paying attention. That brain knows: green discoloration on iron will make a beautiful patina; the glass from a deep blue wine bottle is perfect for Mother Mary's dress. Nothing is too insignificant to scrounge. A tiny bolt may become the baby Jesus on an Annunciation cross. As you transition into this new way of looking, your landscape will change from something you walk hurriedly through to a place where cross material abounds. Your world will transform into a clearer image of a creation where everything, everywhere belongs to God.

Trust your brain— not your analytical mind, but the part of your brain that allows God entry when you aren't paying attention.

Finally, you can turn to the past for your cross-making material. Think of what you own that you don't want to part with: your little girl's baby jewelry, your deceased husband's war medals. How can you honor these times in your past in a meaningful way? If you feel drawn to it, you can dedicate them to God in a cross. The dedication of the war medals will remind you that your husband is now securely with God; the offering of your child's bracelet will repeat the releasing to God that began with her birth. It is symbolic, our giving over to God that which our Sovereign has already given to us. But it is also a definitive act of worship that we are called to do, for "the earth is the Lord's and the fullness thereof" (Ps. 24:1 KJV). What better way to honor this truth than in the form of a cross?

Exercise

There are four primary ways of collecting cross material:

1 Reusing

2 Reclaiming

3 Refocusing

4 Remembering

During the period you have set aside for making crosses, practice a new way of looking at the world:

When you find yourself about to toss something into the garbage, ask yourself: can this be *reused* in a cross?

When you notice that your favorite junk drawer is overflowing with bits and pieces of life, ask yourself: can this be *reclaimed* in a cross?

When you have a beautiful, sunny morning to yourself, *refocus*: Select a parking lot. Grab a canvas collection bag. Set your stopwatch to twenty minutes. Walk the parking lot, head down, scanning your landscape. Collect what you spy. Do not limit yourself to "proper religious colors"—joy comes in all hues. When you're finished, go inside, secure your findings, and wash your hands. Once you've got scrounging down pat, as you walk around in the world, keep your eyes open, telling yourself: "And God saw all that he had made, and it was very good" (Gen. 1:31).

When you have a beautiful, rainy morning to yourself, *remember*: hunt through your closets, your bottom drawers, the boxes in your attic. Collect the mementos of your life and honor them in a cross. These crosses are not just to hang on your wall. They are part of your prayer life. As you sit in meditative prayer, thank God—celebrating and rejoicing in what you have been given.

Notes

8 The Holy Spirit at Work

The materials of cross making are tools for the Holy Spirit to speak to you. You can call them physical symbols or story pieces or whatever you want, but the movement of God will help you put them together. As you assemble the pieces of your cross, don't be surprised if they take you in a direction that is different from what you originally envisioned. That is a really good sign that the Spirit is at work. And don't be surprised if an epiphany moment descends upon you, unexpectedly.

I never know when the epiphany moment in my own cross making will come. Sometimes it appears early, when I've applied the first object to the cross. Sometimes it occurs even earlier, when I'm walking the shoreline and catch sight of the driftwood that so resembles a tree. I immediately know that this driftwood will become The Tree of Life, to represent both the Genesis tree, which offered Adam and Eve the chance to live forever, and the cross of Jesus, which did indeed allow us all to live forever. As I lift the driftwood from the sandy beach, I know that I will make a cross that represents the continuing story of God that began in the Hebrew Bible and has yet

Enter into this spiritual practice,
at all times, as if you are
praying with your hands.

to end, a cross that most dramatically expresses my own view of the cross as the universal symbol of God.

Whenever in the cross making process my flash of understanding arrives—whether at inception, half-way through, or at the tail end—it is, for me, a moment of recognition, not a moment of decision. I suddenly see what God wants me to see, making me feel as if the cross had been just waiting for me to come along and recognize it into existence. Your epiphany moment may strike you the same way. Such remarkable moments are encouraged when you begin and continue your cross making with God uppermost in your mind. Enter into this spiritual practice, at all times, as if you are praying with your hands. What you choose to put on your crosses, what you choose to say with your crosses, and the ways in which you actually construct your crosses, are all ways of talking to, about, and with God. At the same time, God is talking to you and, through you, to others. Cross making is not just decorating two sticks. It is being with God.

When I am engaged in making crosses, my receptivity to God is intensified. New, vibrant insights well up. These religious thoughts arrive not from rumination, but from work. Physical work. Hands messy, arms straining, tongue-poked-out work.

This receptivity is different from the tendency of my Episcopal Church, which is to interact with God cerebrally. Reason—along with Scripture and Tradition—is a cornerstone of our faith. When we engage in Bible study, we sit on folding chairs in a group, reading, talking, offering up our thoughts. When we follow this format, our primary avenue to understanding God is analytical.

Working with crosses makes me long for more. I want something that does not involve reading, study, endless discussion. I want a physical approach to God. A lady preacher told me this physical type of prayer was called "Kinetic prayer." When I researched what Kinetic prayer might be, I saw that she was right: I wanted an understanding that does not come from parsing out an explanation for God, but arrives through a sensory, interactive experience of God. I find such an understanding when my fingers are slimy with glue, mashing papyrus onto driftwood, discovering the hatchmarked strands overlaid into a thick and rough and ancient-looking, fibrous paper. I find it in the dips and bumps of gnarly driftwood. I find it in the rusted contours of picked-up bolts and cast-off nails. I find it in God's world—in all of God's world.

. . . this physical type of prayer was called "Kinetic prayer."

What I have found in this world is that when you are working on creating images of God, God is working on you. Not because you are straining so hard to hear what God has to say, but because you are straining so hard to make this dang thing work. The epiphany comes as swift as a winged bird shooting across the open sky. Understanding zings into your brain and you see something unexpected, enlightening, comforting. Working on God enables God to work on you.

Exercise

Assemble all of your collected items. Spread them in front of you. Finger each one. Meditate on what this item means to you, what that item might mean. Let God come close to you in prayer. The crosses can be quite representational, or the pieces can be put together in a decorative way that shouts, "Hallelujah!" Give it a little bit of time. Let the Holy Spirit work with you and the objects.

Exercise

What "physical" ways have you worshiped God—in dance, drawing, making clay objects? How was that experience different for
you than traditional cerebral worship? If this is your first experience
of engaging in physical spirituality, how does working on your
crosses feel different to you? What would you like to get out of
such a physical prayer experience?

Notes

9 Step Four: Ready for Adornment

Adornment is that which pulls your cross together. It is not the icing on the cake; it is what breathes life into your cross. Before adornment, you have a potential cross. After adornment, you have your story of God told in broken and found objects.

As the Holy Spirit whispers your story to you, you need to follow. Sometimes, you may feel that you are going into a very strange place. You may be following Jesus into the wilderness of the early morning hours, or through the temptations of the devil, or into an understanding that by the standards of this world cannot be right: Am I to die, and die horribly upon a cross? You may feel that the understanding you are working into will make no sense to anyone but you. Quite often, you are wrong. The insight you've been given will be exactly what others in your group need to hear, too. But if the Spirit's whispering is, in fact, for you and you alone, cherish it.

*Let
your mind
relax.
Trust it
to meander
in a
nonlinear
way.*

To get ready for adornment, loosen up. Let your mind relax. Trust it to meander in a nonlinear way. Let the huge conch shell you find on the beach's sandy shores lead you to Jesus' sepulchral tomb. Something inside the conch shell died and left behind the home to which it was attached, only to be tumbled about by massive waves and finally whipped ashore. The shell doesn't need much. A black chunk of driftwood. Nails to depict the piercing of the hands and feet of Jesus, holding him onto the cross. The cross that became his home when he "stretched out his arms upon the cross, and offered himself, in obedience to your will, a perfect sacrifice for the whole world" (*Book of Common Prayer*, 362).

Your collected objects, the movement of your crossbeams, the prayer thoughts that God floats to your brain— they will all come together to create a cross of profound spirituality. Let it happen as God wills.

Exercise

Study the nature of your objects: How would they best be attached to your cross? Do any have holes for dangling? A hollow
middle to be threaded through? Can you hang the object onto
another found object? Sometimes you can slide an object behind
your crosstie. Don't be afraid of leaving things "unglued." This lack
of permanence may be part of the story your cross needs to tell.
The question is, how should you adhere your objects in keeping
with the story you and God are creating? Ponder what the objects
are telling you and let them line up on your cross as they may.

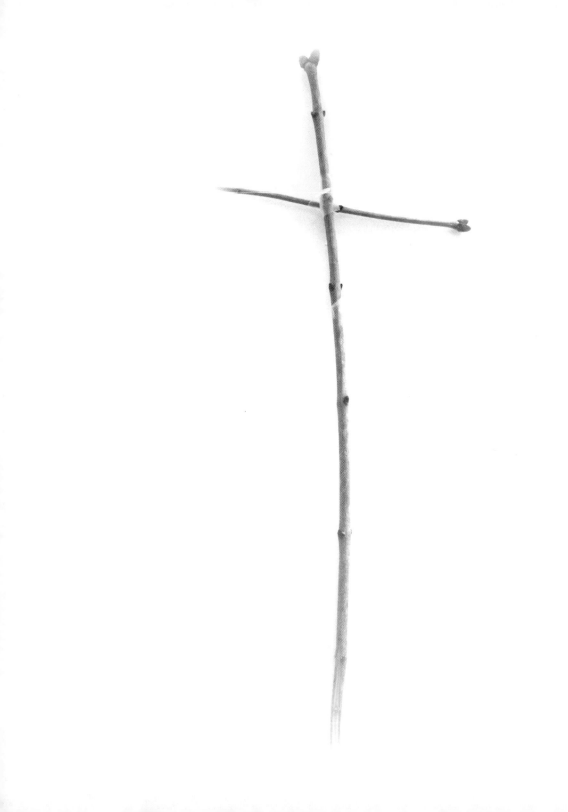

Notes

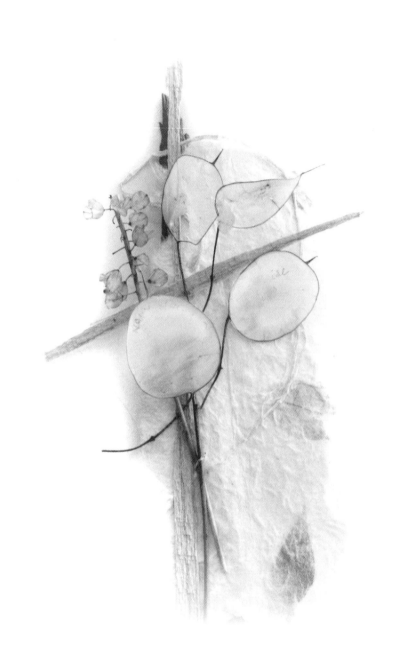

10 Keep Your Eyes on the Cross

It is not our purpose in cross making to create a beautiful cross. Most of the time we do create lovely crosses, but that is the product of following God's leading into a place where we are supposed to be. It is imperative that, as we work, we don't lose sight of our purpose: to focus on God. Make sure in all your activity that your cross doesn't disappear.

I cannot explain on a technical level why a cross will fade into the background, but it can occur in many ways. If, for example, you use as your crosstie the same material that you've used on your mat, the cross will disappear. The eye will light on the crosstie and it will light on the mat. The eye will skip over the cross entirely.

Or if you clutter up your cross up with this thing and that thing— suddenly the cross will be gone. It happens so easily, so unexpectedly, so completely: the cross disappears. Like so many of our churches today that fill their days and nights and weekends with endless programs and activities, your cross may become overwhelmed by activity and details, and the most important aspects of it may disappear.

It isn't
our way.
But it is
God's way.

Why won't that which works in the earthly world work with God? Because it doesn't.

If there is one lesson of the Hebrew Bible, it is that God works differently than we do. God insisted that Abraham send his firstborn son, Ishmael, into the wilderness. God talked Rebecca into instigating the theft of Esau's blessing for the favored one, Jacob. God used a deceptive father to trick Jacob into taking Leah instead of Rachel.

We puzzle over these stories. It isn't right to trick someone out of their blessing. It isn't right to send the firstborn son into the desert. It just isn't right, so, in response, many of us reject these stories in the Hebrew Bible, by ignoring them or feeling somehow that they are no longer relevant to us today. But God doesn't follow the rules that we've happened to work out in our heads; God, ultimately, is not subject to our human explanations.

It isn't our way. But it is God's way.

For God also saved Hagar and Ishmael in the wilderness and made of the lad a great nation. And God reconciled Jacob to Esau in one of the most moving stories of the Hebrew Bible. And God used the birthing competition between Leah and Rachel to create the twelve tribes of Israel.

How do we hear God's way when, through experience and habit, we are so steeped in our own way? The best we can do is to focus on the cross. Take ourselves out of the equation. Keep our ears attuned and our heads cocked in God's direction. Choose a new crosstie and don't pile onto our crosses all that conglomerated clutter. Rethink the whole thing if we have to.

Do whatever is needed. Just make sure the cross doesn't disappear.

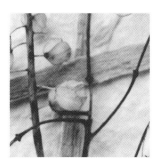

Exercise

Your cross is not a task to be completed. It is an opportunity to be with God. Enjoy that opportunity. Let the meditative nature of your work work on you. Let your cross stretch you in ways you haven't been stretched lately. If something attracts you, ask yourself not just why (i.e., not simply because you like it), but also what my teacher calls the "second why": *why* do you like it? For example, it's not just that you like the color, it's that the color is that of the vestments at Pentecost, and you have been aching for the Holy Spirit to descend into your life. Dig deep to discover what the cross is saying to you.

Notes

11 Step Five:
The Cross Maker at Work

The time while you work on your crosses is special time. Use it to the maximum. If you are working in a group, divide your time into three parts:

1 Talkative time, where you share your thoughts about this new activity;

2 Meditative time, when a member of your group reads from a spiritual text to deepen your cross experience; and,

3 Silent time, when you absorb what God is telling you about your cross.

If there are only two of you working on cross making together, take turns reading from one of your favorite texts. If you are by yourself, read out loud so that your words ring in the air. This is another way to get your spirituality out of your head and into your body: use the lungs and breath that God has given you to vocalize his word for your life. Recognize this as an opportunity to enjoy a

This is another way to get your spirituality out of your head and into your body.

spiritual text that really resonates with you. Spiritual texts can be the Bible, books of poetry, hymns, excerpts from religious writers on Sabbath or prayer or the lives of the saints—anything that will focus your thoughts on listening for God's voice and helping to do God's work.

Silent time is just what it sounds like: at these times, you do not speak. Set a specific length for this silence, no less than ten minutes. For those ten minutes, your thoughts are between you and God. Savor them and incorporate them into the physical activity of your hands. Let time slip by unnoticed until you are called back to the things of this earth.

Give some thought to how you want your quiet time to end. A friend suggested that, for those working in groups, a good way to bring the quiet period to a gentle conclusion is for an appointed person to quietly and slowly begin praying the Lord's Prayer. Another idea is to use the words of John to end quiet time and begin your presentation of your crosses: "In the beginning the Word already was. The Word was in God's presence, and what God was, the Word was. He was with God at the beginning, and through him all things came to be; without him no created thing came into being" (Jn. 1:1–3). Whatever you choose, be as intentional as possible.

The suggested format for your work allows time for what one of my workshop participants called "the nervous chatter" that always accompanies a new experience. This chatter is good. By it, we reassure ourselves. We give ourselves the courage to venture further into what can seem like choppy waters. Then, when we've gotten our "cross legs," so to speak, we are better able to listen to the crafted words that focus our thoughts on a plane higher than how exactly one is supposed to affix a recalcitrant washer to a twig. The quiet time is essential to absorbing all of the above.

Exercise

If you had the opportunity to share with others your favorite
spiritual writings (from books, poems, ancient prayers, or whatever
moves you), what would you choose? Make a list in the Notes
section that follows. When you are working on your crosses by
yourself, after you've gotten underway, stop and enjoy one of your
selected readings. Then return to your cross work.

Notes

12 The Cross Speaks

Over and over again, when people are working on a cross, they will say, "I don't know. Something in this just speaks to me." Of course it does. The cross speaks, and you should listen.

The voice of the cross is quiet but persistent. Usually, with me, the voice has to be persistent because I don't listen the first time it speaks. I will be scanning the cross I'm working on, thinking so much about the task at hand, when my eye snags for a moment on a wrongness. But then it travels on. The snag hardly registers. But somewhere deep inside my brain, it does.

The question is: will I pay attention to it?

If I pay attention to the problem area, I learn something. If I don't, the cross doesn't work, and I learn nothing. In fact, I'm pretty sure that having a cross that works isn't even the main point; the learning is. Because, once you've assimilated that learning, it becomes part of the cross and continues in your life. The working cross becomes a manifestation of that important learning.

The cross speaks, and you should listen.

The little voice calls. I frequently choose to ignore it because whatever God wants me to recognize is bound to be a difficult truth—I don't know how to get the nail to stand up straight! If I listen, however, the nail blossoms into a beautiful rope wound with copper wire, brilliantly glittering.

On the other hand, if I don't try to get to the heart of the matter, if I try to let it slide, my cross won't work. My life won't work. And the One who sends the voice of the cross will weep with sadness at my loss.

Exercise

If your cross isn't quite working, ask yourself honestly: Why not?
How can you fix the awkward part? Will this fix possibly lead to a
deeper, more important cross?

Notes

13 The Importance of Time

Creativity thrives if you give it time. Don't expect it to overwhelm you in one fell swoop. Unless you give it time, you never know what idea is going to turn out good and which will be a loser. You have to keep coming up with the ideas, letting them play out, seeing which way they go, discarding some, keeping others. That's what creativity is: two parts stubbornness, one part flexibility. Give your creativity the time it deserves. After all, even God needed six days to create the world.

Most of the tasks we've lost in this day and age are the repetitive ones that have been replaced by time savers. There is nothing glamorous about hauling heavy loads of laundry to the river to beat the clothes on a rock. I consider this every time I struggle to free the weighted-down, water-soaked cotton robe from the clutches of the washing machine: cleaning our clothing in the past must have been hard physical labor, and good riddance.

But in cross making, repetition glides in like a dove. When you are gluing many, many pieces of broken kitchenware onto a kitchen cross, your soul relaxes if you will allow it to. Consider the process of making papier-mâché frames. Into a mixture of flour, water, and salt, you dip the strips of brown paper bag that you've torn by hand, then run your fingers down the length of the strip, removing the excess and smoothing the goo into the paper so that it is moist and limp. Next, you layer the overlapping strips onto the frame until you've covered it entirely. The frame is finished when the paper dries and you spray a sealant over it. Or you can let the frame dry a little longer and, before you seal it, paint the surface, or work sand into it. Several times I've added lady's stockings or cloth of some sort to the frame material. In many ways, the very slowness of these activities is the point: By putting your hands and brain to work together, with thought-filled care, you slow down long enough to be quiet for a while. Then, you are better able to hear what God would have for you. You can see the type of work involved: repetitive, low-skill, and loosely structured, so as to allow room for spontaneity and creativity, coupled with the intrinsic bonus that what you are ultimately imagining is a way to depict God. For many of us, time is the hardest thing we have to give. But in giving time to your cross, you will regain time. In cross making, time ticks by slowly instead of whizzing by unobserved until we are old, then dead. Make your crosses with Jesus' instructions in your heart:

Do not ask anxiously, "What are we to eat? What are we to drink? What shall we wear?" These are the things that occupy the minds of the heathen, but your heavenly Father knows that you need them all. Set your mind on God's kingdom and his justice before everything else, and all the rest will come to you as well. So do not be anxious about tomorrow; tomorrow will look after itself (Mt. 6:31–34).

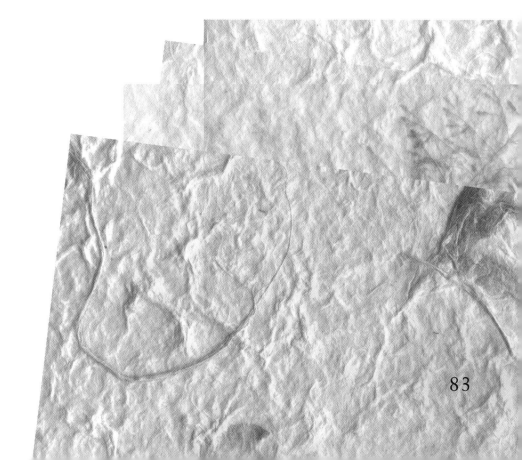

Exercise

When you consider taking the time to make crosses, what do you hear yourself saying in protest? Does it involve your family? Money? Pressing chores? Sayings you received from your parents, teachers, and preachers? Write them down and set them aside. You can pick them back up when your cross is finished.

Notes

14 Step Six: The Story Told by Your Cross

Your cross will tell your story of God. The story will arise from your work; it will be very much your own story. The story is what you are hearing, right now, from the Holy Spirit, and it is very personal. It is immediate. Your cross will probably not tell a Nicene Creed story: "I believe in God the Father . . ." Instead, your cross will probably tell something more like a Lord's Prayer story: "Give us this day our daily bread." When you create that story, you will feel exhilaration, amazement and wonder—at yourself and at God within you. Your pain will ease, understanding will flash into your brain. You will be healed in some way, you will be elated in some way. No matter what, prepare yourself to be delighted by the story of your cross.

People love a story. When describing what I call my "desk" crosses, I've learned to always say that the shells came from the beach where my family has vacationed for thirty years. When people hear that, they know instinctively that it's the beginning of a story. Like little children all dressed for bed, we perk up at the magical, "Once upon a time . . ." We can snuggle into our pillows and relax, thinking, "Oh, this is going to be good."

87

Inside of the story of
your cross
lies the unexpected.

Of course, the original cross story was first told long ago, when our religion was just blooming into being. Told orally, then formed into the written word, the story's plot electrified: our hero was killed by the authorities, then raised triumphantly by none other than God himself. The meaning of the story—that which lies underneath, the deeper meaning—is harder to digest. "Love your neighbor as yourself." "Give up your belongings and follow me." "Seventy times seven if necessary." In all of the stories that my crosses tell about my life, I try to listen and look to hear and understand who I am and who God would have me be.

The word *story* does not mean "fake" or "untrue." It means "narrative," a way of telling that proceeds from first this, then this and finally this. The story of the cross begins with the origin of the cross, how it came into being, way back when. And it proceeds to what it means for all of us. Your crosses—the ones that you make—will tell your spiritual story through the bits and pieces of the materials you use. This story will begin with how your objects began life—a gilded picture frame, a broken ornament, your child's Confirmation cross. But this spiritual story will quickly move into something much deeper: who you are, what God would have you become, and how you are supposed to take up your cross and follow him. As you tell your story in this process, the materials will take on new meaning, for inside of the story of your cross lies the unexpected.

*Bring your life
to God in prayer
as you work.*

Bring your life to God in prayer as you work. You may have really big problems that haven't been fully brought to God before. That's OK. Twists in the plot of any story are essential elements that make a story good: An unwed mother discovers that she is pregnant with the Savior. Or, in a story told by Jesus himself, a wayward son, who has wasted everything his father ever gave him, returns home to a warm embrace and a feast.

Story is as old as the hills and as natural as breathing. Researchers have found through studies that when we take the tragedy of our lives and form it into story, our trauma eases. Story heals. It helps us see past the scattered shrapnel into the beauty of life. We can live without a lot of things. We can live without refrigerators and file cabinets and carpeting on the floor. But we cannot live without story.

At the heart of every good story resides beauty—the beauty of love and death and hope and sacrifice and things not working out at all how you expected, but then the clouds parting, the rays bursting forth, and the finger of God reaching down to the earth to touch, heal, and sear love into our hearts. When you tell the story of your crosses, the story, by necessity, will wind around. That which was the beginning becomes the end. And in the telling of the tale, the answer raised in the beginning lies in the ending:

In the beginning, was the Word, the author of our salvation Jesus Christ.

Come, let me tell you the story of the woman and the lost coin, the shepherd and the lost sheep, the pearl of great value.

Relax, settle in. Let me tell you the never-ending story of the cross . . .

Exercise

Write down the story of your cross. First, identify what has gone into your cross: where the sticks came from, what adornments you used, the origin of your materials. Tell what each object means to you, what it symbolizes. If there is any double meaning in your symbols, explain it. Give your cross a title. Write this story in the Notes section.

Notes

15 Sharing Your Story: The Communality of the Cross

The sharing of our stories is the highlight of the community of the cross. For this reason, it might be most fulfilling to begin your cross-making practice together in a group with others. One of my workshop participants once compared the sharing of our stories to the practice of sharing about lectio divina, where members of a group will share what the Holy Spirit has revealed to them about a particular passage of Scripture.

The father of your storytelling is Jesus: "He told them many things in parables" (Mt. 13:3). "Once there was a man," "A sower went out to sow," "The Kingdom of heaven is like," "A man planted a vineyard." As you tell your story to others, you will be stepping into a long, honorable line of Christian tradition.

Don't be afraid of sharing the story of your cross. It can be intimidating because, if you are honest in your cross making, you will reveal yourself. As you tell the story of your cross, those listening will know what you believe; or at least what you believed at the moment you were creating the cross. They will come to know something about how you feel about your relationship with Christ. What, you might wonder, if I say something that's not quite right? What if my thoughts do not toe the church party line? What if they shake their heads and "tsk, tsk" at me?

In response to our fears, we tend to clam up, taking to heart the advice that it is better to stay silent and appear stupid than to open our mouths and remove all doubt.

But we can't remove all doubt, can we? Step out, and share with others. To make this easier, a good idea is for the group to make a promise to each other that everyone will be heard openly and honestly, without judgment.

No matter how close we come to God in this life, we won't know all of the answers to our questions until we arrive in the next life and finally know. The best we can do is to grope at the glass darkly. I say, "This is the way I see it." And you say, "What about this?" Together, in his name, we approach a place that isn't quite where we were before.

Wouldn't it be wonderful if this willingness to share our stories of God moved beyond our small groups? Maybe it could even catch on. I've already seen groups of people begin to get excited about this new, strange cross-making activity and all of the ideas and emotions that it can generate in people. "It's green, environmentally conscious," some say; others claim it to be the most traditional of practices: taking up our cross. Jesus said, "Anyone who wants to be a follower of mine must renounce self; he must take up his cross and follow me" (Mk. 8:34).

Let's prepare ourselves to engage in a new, different, artistic practice.

Under the umbrella of inclusivity, folks across the country walk with head bent, intent on God's creation, collecting what they once ignored. Crosses of all shapes and sizes begin to emerge: tiny crosses thin as needles, gargantuan crosses lumbering as Godzilla, bread crosses made by bakers, knitted crosses made by knitters, crosses tied with old fishing lures (the "Fishers of Men" cross), crosses quilted by quilters (the "Blessed are the Piecemakers" cross). Each of these crosses has a profound meaning, a way of representing what it means for a particular person to be a child of God. In small groups, inside homes, in the unknown rooms of our hearts, we work on our crosses, rejecting rampant materialism and the monied standards of value and the inexorable panting after more and more. Standing at the crossroads, we choose the path of the cross, and follow into a community of crosses where the people, like the crosses, are all shapes and sizes, hues and complexions. No one talks politics, no one draws lines in the sand, only lines on the cross—wavery, uncertain, very important lines.

I know I have my weaknesses: I buy too many shoes, I fall in love with vintage earrings, I question whether under any circumstances I could voluntarily relinquish my yard—the house, maybe, but the yard? Time and time again, I fall miserably short of where God wants me to be. But in all my brokenness, in my struggling to be found, in my yearning toward God, I am trying to make a cross.

You, too, are trying to make a cross. Together, we will build our crosses, we will share with each other what God means in our lives. And God, in the infinite wisdom that belongs to the Divine, will smile at our handmade, broken, inept gifts of glory.

Exercise

Who will your group of cross makers be? Your Sunday school group? Your neighborhood block group? Your women friends who meet once a month to sip a glass of wine and share time? Your Bible study group? The group at the funky bookstore down the road? Look around you and begin to form your cross making group.

Notes

Part 2
Other Things You Might Want to Know

16 The Joy of Themes

I love a theme. Parties are great with themes. Clothes are great with themes. Life is great with themes. And so are crosses. Themes can be of place—the neighborhood community center where all of your materials are collected, for example—with the cross dedicated to that particular place. Themes can be of time, such as crosses created during a weekend retreat. Themes can be seasonal, either our worldly seasons or the church's holy calendar, such as "Lent into Easter" crosses (arrange your cross made of tree branches in a bowl of water and pebbles; see if the cross will bloom for Easter). If you select a theme such as "Joy," or "Praise and Thanksgiving," or "Sacrifice," it will give you parameters. Similar to the discipline of form in classical poetry, a theme can help release your creativity.

> *See,*
> *that's the thing*
> *about the crosses:*
> *while you are*
> *working on them,*
> *they are working*
> *on you.*

Themes can challenge you in ways you don't expect. My cousin's wife once gave me both the theme for a cross I was to make for her, and the broken shards of her grandmother's vase to use in the making.

"I broke my grandmother's vase," she said, sitting with me on the deck at the beach. "Could you make a cross out of that?"

I told her I'd love to try.

"And I want my theme to be acceptance," she said. "I need to be more accepting of people. If you made a cross on acceptance, I could hang it on the wall and each time I walked by, I would think about accepting people better."

There, in the twilight of the evening with the day's sun tingling on our skin and the moon rising over the phosphorescent waves, it all sounded so lovely: a commissioned cross using a beloved vase to represent a requested theme. Wasn't this the type of activity that made cross making worthwhile?

Then the vase fragments arrived in the mail. The vase was Christmas china, decorated with images of holly leaves. I would never use that in a cross. What was I going to do? I was going to make a cross with that vase, that's what.

106

And it hit me: that's what acceptance is. Accepting others' tastes, their loves, their wants and desires—and forgetting about yours. Working off what they have, trying to do the best for them. Them, them, them—not you, you, you.

Acceptance. See, that's the thing about the crosses: while you are working on them, they are working on you.

Just like so many things in life where we think we are the one who is doing—washing the old lady's hair, hauling sod for the Habitat for Humanity house—it turns out that we are the one being done upon. With this shifting in our understanding, we unblock something inside ourselves: hubris, condescension, our pride in our charitable heart. The removal of this blockage is what allows the kingdom of God to appear. Not the doing unto others, but as you would have them do unto you. The power of the Holy Spirit preached by Jesus and given by God is what connects us all one to another inside the kingdom.

Exercise

Make some themed crosses. Stroll around your church parking lot and then make a cross only from things you find there. Take a Sunday afternoon to make a Sabbath cross. Let a word that keeps popping into your head during prayer time—*forgiven, devotion, abandonment*—become your theme. Work with your theme, listen to your hands as they reveal what God wanted you to hear.

Notes

17 The Value of Gifts

There is one exception to the rule that my crosses are made of materials that have no worldly value: items that are gifted. Some of the things I receive are truly special. Old medals, rings, silver crosses. Even the world would see these items as having value in and of themselves. To me, the true value lies in the fact that someone gave it to me. "I can't use this anymore and don't know what to do with it," she says, and donates it to the cross. Isn't that wonderful—that something the world would covet is instead donated to the cross?

Let the word get out that you make crosses from broken and found objects and see what God rolls your way. I've been given stones from a child's field trip to the petrified forest; they became the steps of a "Wilderness Cross." A statue smashed by a Down syndrome child became a plea to "Pray for the World." At one of my husband's monthly church meetings, a parishioner handed him a single earring and told him it was for me to use in my cross making. My aunt sent me costume jewelry from the 1950s, strands of big clunky bronze beads. A writer friend gave me her used-up fountain pen. My mother—who drops, breaks, and smashes various things on a regular basis—brought me a juice glass of the most delicate yellow hue.

In God's eyes, we are, all of us, "broken and found."

I love to see gifts embedded in a cross. It's as if a piece of a person I love has become part of the cross. What once had belonged to them is now transformed. The people who give me their broken things tell me that knowing there's a path that leads elsewhere than the garbage can comfort them when something is broken. It helps to know the thing once loved will be used in a cross.

This is the same reaction we have when our lives are broken, smashed by unexpected things beyond our control or by our own hands. We cry out, we hang our heads. Then we remember: God can use this. In God's eyes, we are, all of us, "broken and found." We are transformed by the love that saved, offered, and gave itself to us.

Exercise

Let folks know that you are making crosses from broken and found objects. Solicit their contributions. In fact, why not try making a cross entirely of gifted items. Wouldn't that truly be a body of Christ cross?

Notes

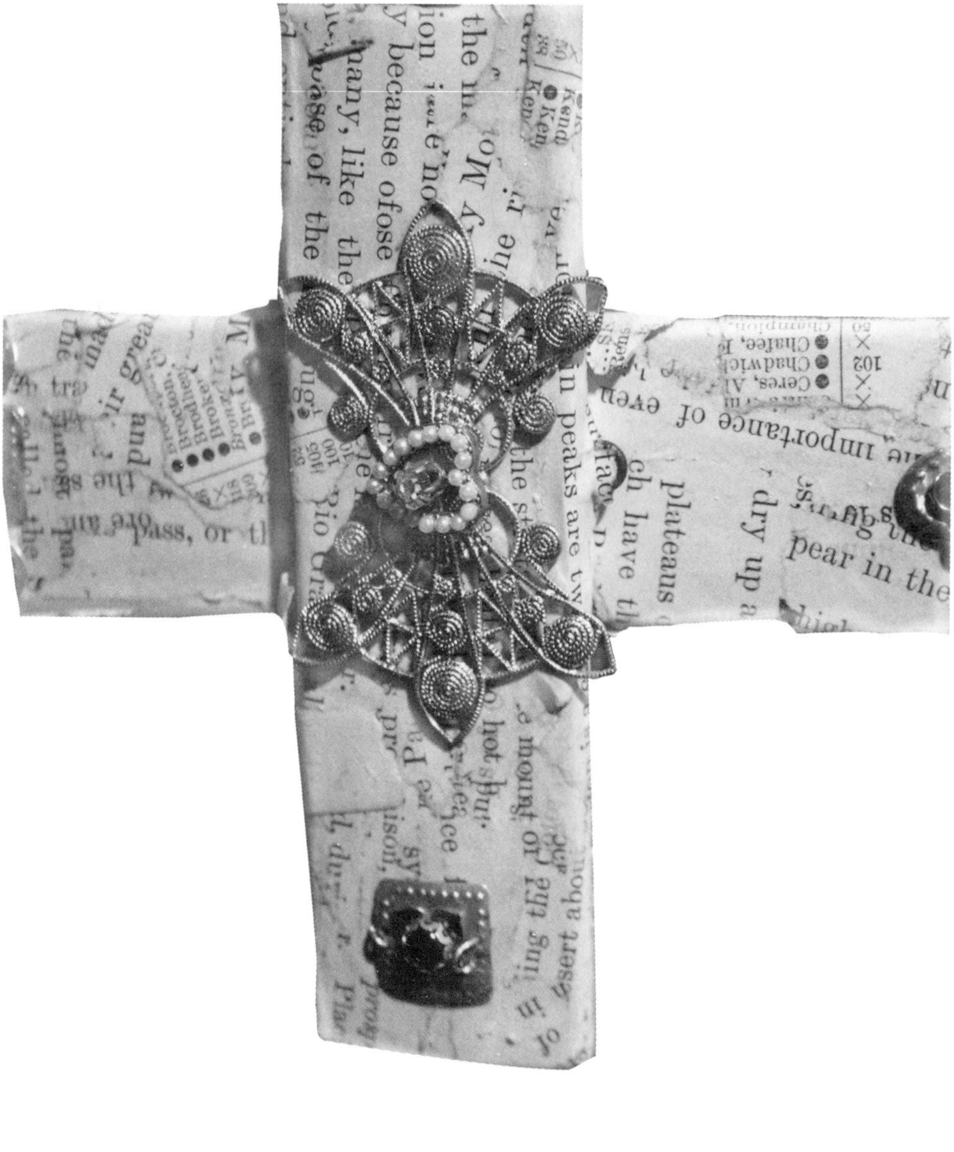

pass, or
peaks are tw
plateaus
dry up a
pear in the

18 What to Do with Your Crosses

You may wonder what to do with all of these crosses you make. I'm so glad you asked. There are wonderful ways to honor your cross, either through loving treatment in your own home or by finding new homes for them:

Hold a cross festival where you sell your handmade crosses. Give the money you raise to "the least of these" (Mt. 25:40 KJV).

Offer the crosses as condolence gifts—the cross comforts people every day in God's mysterious ways, and handmade crosses are great vehicles of this comfort.

Make a cross room in your house and fill it with your crosses. Fill your stairwell with crosses. Fill whatever is empty with crosses. Tell people about your crosses and what they mean when they visit. Give one away whenever it seems to "speak" to someone.

Give a cross.

Give the crosses away at Christmas time or better yet, give one to each child who is baptized in your church this Easter.

Let a new priest in your church pick out a cross as a special ordination gift.

Attach small crosses to packages as an extra gift. Encourage the recipients to talk with you about them.

Give a cross to each member of your Bible study group to celebrate the occasion of being together.

Hang a cross over your home altar—meditate on it in your prayer time.

Give crosses away as housewarming gifts.

Give crosses as hostess gifts: what better gift for a beach house than a driftwood cross?

Give crosses as graduation gifts; when children go into the wider world, they need to take a cross with them.

Hang crosses on your Christmas tree to remember the meaning of the season.

If your cross is made with natural materials, such as driftwood or strands of grapevine, hang the cross outdoors or on your porch.

Whenever someone does something unexpected that releases the Holy Spirit into the world, thank them and give them a cross that you've made specially for them.

If a cross is narrow and made of copper wire, use it as a bookmark in your Bible.

If a cross is small and metallic, wear it on a necklace, close to your heart.

Make a cross that fits into the palm of your hand and lay it on your desk so that you can grab it during the workday when things seem overwhelming.

Do with your cross what comes to you—it will be the right thing.

Do with your cross what comes to you— it will be the right thing.

Exercise

What have you done with your crosses? Visit my website and contact me at www.makingcrosses.com and I'll share your ideas with others.

Notes

19 The Never-Ending Cross

We have come to the end. There is so much more to say—I want to tell you about the joy of making crosses with children; I want you to know more about kitchen crosses hung in kitchen windows over kitchen sinks; and have I told you about the women who wear their crosses, carrying them throughout the day? I could go on forever, and I hate endings, anyway. Except with the cross, the story never ends, not altogether.

If at all possible, get your crosses into the world. With your family, your friends, in any way you can. Use the ideas in the previous chapter as your starting point. Over the years, I have come to realize that cross creations are made alive by the attention of others. You will find that they are great conversation starters. If you have always had trouble talking about your faith and yet would like to, wear one of the crosses that you've made. You will find your cross is a natural opening to talk about your faith and what this symbol means to you.

Those who gaze upon a cross (and gazing is perfectly normal and OK, by the way) begin to learn something about it, and the greater Something that it represents. Those who share their feelings with you after seeing one of your crosses participate in the creation of that cross and, perhaps, of another one yet to come. The story the cross presents becomes not what you might have intended, but what they see within its finished form . . . but not really finished until someone else enters in. Like my friend who looked at my "Rebecca" cross, with its blank space where Isaac might have been, and wondered about it. I told her the space was intentional, "Because he is such a non-actor in the story." "And he was blind," she said. The crosses are not finished until someone else brings their own vision to them.

Sometimes I feel a twinge when I realize that a cross I've made is no longer mine. This cross that came into being under the work of my hands and rested on my dining room table and offered itself up on the charity auction table will never be mine again.

Then I remember the words of Christ: "I will not leave you bereft; I am coming back to you" (Jn. 14:18). So, letting crosses go, just like learning to let go of all things so that God can be in control, is what we're supposed to do. And we know, "I am coming back to you."

*Get your crosses
into the world.*

Exercise

Say goodbye to your cross. Even if you merely hang it on your study wall, the cross will no longer be yours and yours alone. Those who come into your house will ask about your cross; they will tell you what they see in this, your cross. After that, your eyes won't see the cross in the same way. It will then contain not only the parts of this world that you have used to make it—it will contain part of the body of Christ as well.

Notes

Appendix
Supplies and Tips
for Individuals and Groups

Supplies

LIST OF SUPPLIES	ADDITIONAL SUPPLIES
	(if desired)
Sticks	Twine or string
Wire, light gauge, any color	Raffia
Scissors	Fishing wire
Tissue paper	Baby wipes
Elmer's glue	Latex gloves to protect your hands
Water	from glue
Small bowls to hold watered glue	Glue dots
Bags for collecting objects	Needle and thread
Found objects	Hammer and nails
Multisurface glue	Scrap fabric
Toothpicks to smear glue	Sealant, glossy or matte finish
Wet paper towels for sticky hands	Butcher paper to protect work
	tables from dripping glue
	Needle-nose pliers for pulling wire

Tips

A. TIPS FOR EVERYONE

Verbal Prayer

It's always good to open and close each workshop session with a prayer. It sets your mind, as well as the "mind" of the group, in the right place.

Proper Cross Material

All material created by God's hand is proper cross material. If you feel odd using something on a cross, remind yourself: everything was made by God's hand.

Methods of Adhesion

Needle and Thread: You can "thread" your needle with wire, twine, or anything that will fit through the eye. An embroidery needle gives you a bigger eye and more options.

Hammer and Nails: Some nails—such as copper roofing nails or carpet tacks—are decorative and very symbolic on a cross, but they will not hold anything together. Other nails actually work.

Glue: Pick the glue appropriate for your job. If using a heavy-duty glue, wear gloves and use a toothpick to dab it into place. Immediately wash off any glue that gets on your skin. Hot glue does not last. It is for convenience, not permanence. Sooner or later, anything hot-glued will fall off. A better choice is to use one of the all-purpose glues that dry clear, carried by most hardware stores; I would recommend that you select a glue that is labeled non-toxic.

Wire: Wire comes in various gauges, from light to heavy, and can be made of many different materials, in many different colors—silver, brown, copper, green, and others. Wire can be purchased at a hardware store, a florist, or at the dollar store.

Twine: A ball of twine is an excellent thing to have in your supplies. Twine is symbolic of the sheep, the pasture, the Shepherd in biblical imagery. You can collect both twine and raffia off many packagings given to you when you shop.

Finishing

Don't worry about the backside of your cross until the very end. Then twist and turn the cross from all directions to fill in holes.

Design

If you know that you want to hang your cross on the wall, work small wire hangers into the design of it.

Matting and Framing

The pine stretchers that artists use to stretch their canvases work well as frames for your crosses. The stretchers are mitered, with grooves to slip the pieces together. They come in different sizes; you can assemble any shape frame you want. Snug the pieces together and cover them in papier-mâché. Then paint or decorate the frame any way you want.

If you decide to frame your cross, you may need a mat. It's best not to use paper as a cross mat. Even in normal indoor light, the color on the paper will fade. Hang the cross anywhere near sunlight and the fading will be so strong, you'll end up with a shadow outline.

To secure a heavy cross to a backing, poke a hole in the backing and "sew" the cross on using a large-eyed embroidery needle and wire.

Special Times of the Year

You may want to select a time period for working on crosses, such as Lent or Advent. These special times of the church year can be the best occasions for focusing your attention on the life of Christ and the meaning of the Cross. These crosses can be made by church groups, such as Sunday School classes, where each meeting, a little more work is done on the cross. My church made a red plywood Pentecost cross during Fellowship Hour one summer. If you find yourself making crosses by yourself, set up a card table with your supplies in a room where they are least likely to be bothered. Spend a little bit of time each day on the cross. Don't worry about leaving it "undone" each day. Leave it and return. Build your cross over the length of time that you've set aside for the practice.

B. TIPS FOR WORKSHOP LEADERS

Preparation of the Room

* When possible, arrange your work tables in a circle or square, so participants can face each other.
* Cover the tables in sheets of butcher paper or something similarly sturdy, to protect from dripping glue.

Making Your Crossbeams

* If your time is limited wrap your sticks into crossbeams before your participants arrive. During the workshop, have the participants focus on selecting the particular sticks that seem to be the ones for them.
* If your participants will be making their own crossbeams at the workshop, count on needing several twelve-inch-long lengths of wrapping wire per person, plus wire for adhering objects to the cross.
* If you are using tissue paper to decorate the crossbeams, allow the participants to mix their own glue and water, if possible (see Chapter Six for directions on using the tissue paper).
* If your group is working with natural objects, you will likely not need to decorate the crosses with tissue paper. Tissue paper provides a needed background to metal and manmade, found objects; but objects from nature provide their own color and texture.

Collection

* If possible, in your promotional literature on the workshop, encourage participants to bring found objects of their own to the workshop.
* If your workshop is only planned for one session, you will need to have a box of collected objects ready for participants to use, in addition to whatever someone might bring in. If you have many objects, sort them by color to help the participants begin the choosing process.
* If your group is collecting objects from nature, remind your participants not to fear impermanence. The materials they collect may wither within three days, but that's okay. The cross is about now.

Adornment

* If you have brought in a box of objects, let participants look through the box and select those things they want to use. Depending on your number of participants, you will probably want several boxes circulating so everyone can be engaged at once. Encourage the participants to allow the Holy Spirit to guide their selection without knowing exactly why they are choosing what they choose.
* You may want to read for the group a few Bible verses on the role of the Holy Spirit, to open the session. For example:

    Jesus said: "The Advocate, the Holy Spirit, whom the Father will send in my name, will teach you everything, and remind you of all that I have said to you" (Jn. 14:26).

131

"Do you not know that your body is a temple of the Holy Spirit within you, which you have from God, and that you are not your own?" (1 Cor. 6:19)

"These things God has revealed to us through the Spirit; for the Spirit searches everything, even the depths of God" (1 Cor. 2:10).

* Once everyone has selected their objects, follow the sectioning of time set out in Chapter 11. If your workshop is formed on a theme, during the time of spiritual reading, you can read your themed material. As to the quiet time, your participants may not like it at first, but they will thank you afterward for the time of reflection.

* Encourage trial and error. Hold an object up to the cross and see how it looks. Replace it if you don't like it.

* Make available a Bible, hymnal, prayer book, and other resources for people in case a passage comes to them as they work and they want to look up the full text.

Telling the Story of Your Cross

*Always leave plenty of time for the sharing of the cross stories; it is everyone's favorite part.

* Sharing should always be completely optional. It is still cross making if it is for no one but the cross maker.

*As the crosses are shared, remind your participants that everyone began with the same basic materials. The difference between the crosses comes from their working with God.

About Paraclete Press

Who We Are

Paraclete Press is a publisher of books, recordings, and DVDs on Christian spirituality. Our publishing represents a full expression of Christian belief and practice—from Catholic to Evangelical, from Protestant to Orthodox.

We are the publishing arm of the Community of Jesus, an ecumenical monastic community in the Benedictine tradition. As such, we are uniquely positioned in the marketplace without connection to a large corporation and with informal relationships to many branches and denominations of faith.

What We Are Doing

Paraclete Press Books | Paraclete publishes books that show the richness and depth of what it means to be Christian. Although Benedictine spirituality is at the heart of all that we do, we publish books that reflect the Christian experience across many cultures, time periods, and houses of worship. We publish books that nourish the vibrant life of the church and its people.

We have several different series, including the best-selling Paraclete Essentials and Paraclete Giants series of classic texts in contemporary English; Voices from the Monastery—men and women monastics writing about living a spiritual life today; award-winning poetry; best-selling gift books for children on the occasions of baptism and first communion; and the Active Prayer Series that brings creativity and liveliness to any life of prayer.

Mount Tabor Books | Paraclete's newest series, Mount Tabor Books, focuses on liturgical worship, art and art history, ecumenism, and the first millennium church; and was created in conjunction with the Mount Tabor Ecumenical Centre for Art and Spirituality in Barga, Italy.

Paraclete Recordings | From Gregorian chant to contemporary American choral works, our recordings celebrate the best of sacred choral music composed through the centuries that create a space for heaven and earth to intersect. Paraclete Recordings is the record label representing the internationally acclaimed choir Gloriæ Dei Cantores, praised for their "rapt and fathomless spiritual intensity" by *American Record Guide*; the Gloriæ Dei Cantores Schola, specializing in the study and performance of Gregorian chant; and the other instrumental artists of the Gloriæ Dei Artes Foundation.

Paraclete Press is also privileged to be the exclusive North American distributor of the recordings of the Monastic Choir of St. Peter's Abbey in Solesmes, France, long considered to be a leading authority on Gregorian chant.

Paraclete Video | Our DVDs offer spiritual help, healing, and biblical guidance for a broad range of life issues including grief and loss, marriage, forgiveness, facing death, bullying, addictions, Alzheimer's, and spiritual formation.

Learn more about us at our website:
www.paracletepress.com or phone us
toll-free at 1.800.451.5006

SCAN
TO
READ
MORE

Discover the "Active Prayer Series"

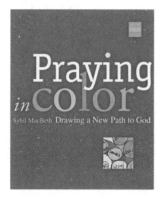

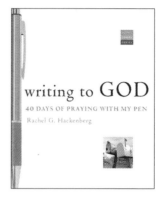

Sybil MacBeth
ISBN: 978-1-55725-512-9; $17.99 Paperback

Rachel G. Hackenberg
ISBN: 978-1-55725-879-3; $15.99 Paperback

"Just as Julia Cameron, in *The Artist's Way*, showed the hardened Harvard businessman he had a creative artist lurking within, MacBeth makes it astonishingly clear that anyone with a box of colors and some paper can have a conversation with God. Readers of all ages, experience and religions will find this a fresh, invigorating and even exhilarating way to spend time with themselves and their Creator."
—*Publishers Weekly*

"Hackenberg's words have a heartbeat—sometimes they are beautiful and otherworldly; other times they are simple and earthy. When I read her prayers, I'm sure I have just prayed. But she wants me to take up *my* pen and pray. With a prayer, a Scripture passage, and a task, she gives me a personal invitation and permission to enter the incarnational practice of writing my words to God."
—Sybil MacBeth, author of *Praying in Color: Drawing a New Path to God*

Available from most booksellers or through Paraclete Press
www.paracletepress.com; 1-800-451-5006
Try your local bookstore first.

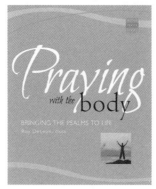